Reflections Of His Glory

(52 Inspirational Majestic Reflections)

J. K. Sanchez

Reflections of His Glory (52 Inspirational Majestic Reflections)
ISBN -13: 978-0692532270
ISBN – 10: 0692532277

Copyright © 2015 by J. K. Sanchez.
Published by: Button Lane Books Spanaway, WA 98387
Contact: Judy@jksanchez.com - www.jksanchez.com

Cover Photography by:
Majestic Reflection-J.K.Sanchez Photography
Cover Design by:
ButtonLaneBooks : www.buttonlanebooks.com

Dedication

To those who have begun and continue to walk on this narrow path of stepping into a life journey of pursuing the presence of our Lord Jesus Christ above all other life distractions. Enjoy the journey as you bask in the reflections of His Glory and spend time at His feet!

Contents

Introduction ix

Winter's Rest

Taking New Territory...............................1
Desire for a Single Drop of New Wine..............2
Blanket of Peaceful Purity..........................4
The Deep Roots of Victorious Conquerors...........6
His Creative Forces................................8
The Choice – To Mount Up with Wings
    Like Eagles...................................9
A Life Lived on the Hamster Wheel? Or
    Have You "Gone Fishing"?...................11
Go To The Mountains vs Go To
    The Mattresses.............................13
The Seasons of Our Lives – A Different Way
    Of Thinking (Part 1 – Fall)................16
The Seasons of Our Lives – A Different Way
    Of Thinking (Part 2 – Winter)..............18
The Seasons of Our Lives – A Different Way
    Of Thinking (Part 3 – Spring)..............19
The Seasons of Our Lives – A Different Way
    Of Thinking (Part 4 – Summer)..............20
Cinderella and the Bride of Christ................22

Spring's Assurance

Winter's Thaw – "Some People Are Worth
Melting For".........................27
The Fog Veil Was Torn......................29
Silencing the Voices of Winter.................32
Step Over the Threshold or Slam the Door.........34
Creations Explosion of
New Life and Promise!..............37
Ready to Run Before the Wind...................39
The Beauty of First Flight – Believe You Are
Made For More......................43
Be Who You Were Created To Be!.................45
Life Giving Presence – The River..................47
Mission Possible...............................49
No Worries – Just Sing..........................51
Encouragement Brings New Life.................52
"With This Ring".............................53

Summer's Delight

The Beauty of a Bleeding Heart...................57
No Weeds, No Fences in the Kingdom.............59
Blooming In His Love..........................61
The Growth Process of a Seed....................63
Summer's Stirring of Our Senses
The Gift of Sight!...................65
The Gift of Sound!.................67
The Gift of Taste!.................69
The Gift of Touch!.................71
The Gift of Smell!.................74

Transformation Awaits – Just Jump 76
Hesitant, Confident or "Sold-Out" Jumper?............78
Float the Center of the River...................81
We Are His Chosen Stones...................83

Fall's Yield

"There's No Place Like Home"...................87
Decisions on the Yellow Brick Road...............89
Freedom Flows Under His Reign...............91
Nature's Nudging...................93
Nature's Surrender
      The Last Lonely leaves...................95
      Those "Holding On" to Full Color...........99
      Early Yielders...................101
The Woodpeckers Single Focus...................102
Yield to the Call and Open the Door...............104
Let Him Sweep Up the Mess...................106
Believe in His Faithfulness...................108
Abundant Fruit Happens in a Yielded Life...........110
The Faithful Evergreen's Canopy...................112

Acknowledgments

First and foremost, I am thankful for the support and consistent overflow of love from my husband, Dennis, my children, their spouses and my grandchildren. My overwhelming Joy is found in each of your faces.

My continued love and appreciation to my sister, my friend, my almost TWIN in every way and <u>my editor</u>. Thank you Donna for always being there and knowing my thoughts before I speak them. Without you there would have been MANY mistakes.

And finally – but above all – my thanks to Jesus Christ who directed, inspired, and taught me (step by step) to enjoy the journey. His presence and promise of favor and abundance are always there for me. **My life is not my own but a gift freely given back to the one who gave His life for me.**

Introduction

My passionate journey for the presence of the Lord began within me decades ago and has drawn me to a narrow path filled with promise and freedom that I have never experienced before. During this journey I have found a deep <u>knowing</u> of my true identity as a daughter of the King and His amazing love for ME. As my path has narrowed to a place of the <u>one thing</u> – His face and presence - I have learned a new depth of love, rest, contentment and delight. These have shown me the importance of simplification that has brought me true freedom in Christ, as He has become Lord of my life.

His gift on the cross is just that – a gift. All of the "I can do's" are learning to lie down as my life is becoming focused on Him and what has already been "done" for me.

This book has been ignited directly from that love and I desire to share, direct and encourage you to a place to meet Him, love Him, hear Him, see Him and be a lover of His presence as I am.

ENJOY THIS AMAZING JOURNEY OF BASKING IN HIS GLORY!

Winter's Rest

Taking New Territory

Each time you begin a new year, a new job, a new relationship etc. you have been given an opportunity to walk into new territory. A whole new place in which you can expect to see dreams fulfilled, long awaited changes to occur and promises come to pass.

During the colonial enterprises, the Samurai would often plant a cherry blossom tree to symbolize a victory where territory was taken.

Your new beginning has sprung forth with expectation of territory to be won.

The past is gone.

Your victory has been won as you accept the undeserved gift purchased for you on the cross of Jesus Christ.

Your choice is simply to accept that gift (your planted Cherry Tree) and leave the past failures and hurts behind. This victory then allows you to freely walk into your new territory with expectation of new fulfillment of promises.

Join me and step with victory out of past failure into all that He has planned for you. Plant your cherry blossom tree and take that new territory.

Desire for a Single Drop of New Wine

With the desire for just a single drop of new wine comes the understanding that there is a process of change that must occur.

The old wine skin with its past taste and presence of old wine must be cast off to allow a new supple skin to be prepared.

With desire comes acceptance and anticipation of this new wine. The joy that will come from that one drop of wine as it touches your tongue stirs within. All the past doesn't compare to that desire, making the cast off process an easy choice.

This new skin is now ready to receive, expand and contract as the new flavor begins. An amazing fragrance begins to bubble up from within - allowing the fermentation to occur.

The sweetness of this coming new wine continues the maturing process as it rests, breathing in and out allowing pressure to grow and release.

The excitement of a new sweet taste begins to grow, along with an aroma that is beginning to swirl within. Excitement and anticipation begin to erupt within this new wine skin as the wine changes and is ready to be poured out.

The time to taste has arrived and with it comes a cry of exhilaration from your heart.

Your heart sings out "Just one single drop is more than enough"

But the skin bulging with fragrant sweetness has done its work and pours forth a release within you that erupts in a joy of transformation as the new wine saturates not only you but also the very atmosphere that surrounds you.

Join me as you begin to desire the exciting changes to come - the casting off of old wineskins as well as a renewed hunger and thirst for more of His presence.

Matthew 9:17 - Neither is new wine put into old wineskins. If it is, the skins burst and the wine is spilled and the skins are destroyed. But new wine is put into fresh wineskins, and so both are preserved.

Psalm 63:1 - O God, you are my God; earnestly I seek you; my soul thirsts for you; my flesh faints for you, as in a dry and weary land where there is no water.

<u>Blanket of Peaceful Purity</u>

Snowflakes begin to fall and with them amazing change appears. They start to build up and bring quietness to the air. Accumulating they begin to lay a blanket over the landscape. This silent white blanket of flakes brings a peace and contentment that settles over the entire atmosphere.

Where barrenness, clutter, filth and decay may have once reigned only moments before now a pure blanket lies quietly upon them, covering the once chaotic scene. Before your eyes the change occurs and these changes bring change within your own spirit. Peace falls - contentment begins to find home and rest reigns, even if for a short time.

Often there are parallels between nature and the spiritual.

As I contemplate the quiet scene that is materializing and the change of atmosphere before me I see how barrenness, clutter, filth and decay are carried within.

If you open your heart and allow access to Jesus, He will bring purity like the snow. When He comes you are promised not a covering of all your decay that will melt away but a complete obliteration of your internal decay that will change the atmosphere in you and around you.

4

When that obliteration comes the amazing gift of the Holy Spirit comes in like a flood – cleansing and changing you. The permanent promise of peace, contentment, rest and freedom materializes in your life as you walk in His presence through Christ.

Just as nature responds with acceptance of this blanket of peaceful purity you too can accept the free gift of His forgiveness to obliterate your decay and walk in a place of peace, forever at rest.

The Deep Roots of Victorious Conquerors

As I sit silently absorbing the beauty of the trees around me I am drawn once more into contemplation of the enormity of my Heavenly Fathers creative design.

The most interesting thought and spiritual parallel is found in the very roots beneath these trees, of which we never see but without them they could never complete the plan and design that God had created them for.

The trees that are the strongest, those who weather the toughest storms and produce the most fruit have strong deep roots.

Deep roots are pursued in the quite unseen places of the earth. They are made stronger over years of endurance as they press down through soil, clay and rock searching for the deep water.

Those that find the deep water gain refreshment while others are withering. These are those that survive the droughts of heat-parched ground and survive the strongest winds that pound and bend them almost to the ground. Here they continue to stand tall, solid and are ready to fight the next battle.

These are the same that stand as the strongest towers, the front lines of the storms. They stand as protectors and guards for many others.

These tenacious towers find strength from the deep water beneath. Their roots support and hold strong to that unseen faith in the position of their taproot. They continually draw from the deep unseen river.

Our understanding and continual revelation of Jesus Christ as our taproot determines our root system, our trees purpose and plan and the ability to stand as one with deep roots. We can be one who comes through the battle victorious - still standing as a conqueror.

It's that deep unseen root system and faith that will allow this tree to grow to its full purpose.

Jeremiah 17:8 - He is like a tree planted by water, that sends out its roots by the stream, and does not fear when heat comes, for its leaves remain green, and is not anxious in the year of drought, for it does not cease to bear fruit.

Romans 8:37 - No, in all these things we are more than conquerors through him who loved us.

His Creative Forces

We all walk in a world of pressure imposed on us from our circumstances, others demands and internal unfulfilled expectations. How we respond to those pressures can cause us to grow and become like that beautiful life giving waterfall or the destructive force of a volcano.

In nature pressure also does both; creates beauty or destruction - pearls, diamonds and waterfalls as well as earthquakes and volcanoes.

Pearls and diamonds are created in a place of pressure where stillness and time are the Creator's force. Waterfalls are created from a constant movement to a place of freedom that erupts with the joyful sound of release.

Just like the creative force behind the pearl and diamond we can walk through pressures resting in the knowledge that through Christ "He's got our back" - and with that comes a freedom and joyful release of pressures like the waterfall.

Walking through daily pressures in this way will create a thing of beauty and transform you from "glory to glory".

It's your choice what you want those pressures to create - beauty or destruction.

The Choice – To Mount Up with Wings Like Eagles

The majestic Eagle depends on his physical design; strength, speed and sharp vision for his survival. Just as the Eagle does, so do we often depend on the "I" of our abilities.

There comes a time to the Eagle where a molting process must be faced. This process brings this majestic proud bird to a weakened position. His feathers, strength, vision and ability to fly or hunt are eliminated during this time of preparation for renewal.

We too, come to this place; where all of what "I" can do and what "I" have done are no longer of value. We then face a choice, a choice of the heart. A choice that requires a willingness to give up all of what "I" can do and trust in what "He" did for us at the cross.

The Eagles too must make a similar choice. Many roll over and die choosing the memory of the "I" of their former majesty. Those who are renewed are those who turn to the sun, rest and wait. They then are restored not to the former majesty but to a stronger and greater one.

We too can only reach new heights with renewed vision and strength when our eyes are on the "Son" not the "I". Only then can His plans, purposes and design for our life be renewed.

Trust that His plans for you are far greater then your "I" plans. So chose today to learn from the renewed Eagle. Join me and look to the Son - Rest and Wait.

Isaiah 40:31 — but they who wait for the Lord shall renew their strength; they shall mount up with wings like eagles; they shall run and not be weary; they shall walk and not faint.

A Life Lived On the Hamster Wheel? or

Have You "Gone Fishing"?

As a type "A" personality I've spent most of my life seeing my life either as a juggler trying to keep all the plates spinning at the same time or as the constantly running hamster on the wheel. This was just who I was - or so I thought.

One day as my "people pleasing" "self imposed" spinning plates began to crash around me; I ranted out my frustration to God, hoping He would help me keep them going. However, that day I found that God has a sense of humor. In the midst of my tirade a minds eye picture flashed into my head. A painted board with the words "Gone Fishing" presented itself. My reaction quickly turned from startled to an uncontrollable laughter. I knew this was His direct answer to that prayer.

Embracing that thought, stopping the craziness, getting off the wheel, living it and walking it has taken me on a journey of finding the person I was designed to be.

In the resting and "going fishing" process, enjoyment of life begins to dawn as relief and freedom become possible. Trusting Jesus, His plan for your life and daily walking in a place of rest are all part of this growth.

Does everything get done? Nope. Does it matter? Nope. Do you lose friends? YES. Some of those you were constantly trying to please, those who kept you on the wheel due to their expectations but not ones that matter. Is it easy? Nope. Is it worth it? Oh Yes. It brings a clear focus of what is important in your life, brings new meaning and crystallizes your focus on who you were designed to be.

Join me in this amazing process. Get off the wheel. Take time to embrace, rest, and trust in Christ's unique design that is who you are. Enjoy going fishing.

Matthew 11:28-30 - Come to me, all who labor and are heavy laden, and I will give you rest. Take my yoke upon you, and learn from me, for I am gentle and lowly in heart, and you will find rest for your souls. For my yoke is easy, and my burden is light.

Go To The Mountain

vs Go To The Mattresses

We all have a tendency to either go to the mountain or go to the mattresses as decisions are made in our lives.

Both mean you are preparing for a new direction, purpose, plan or battle. You are willing to risk it all to get there. It's just the approach that varies and that approach transforms you.

Which do you lean toward?

Both Jesus and Moses went to the Mountain.

Both were seeking strength, encouragement and direction for the task ahead.

Jesus met with Elijah and Moses, who prepared him for what was to come, their presence brought strength, encouragement and Gods manifest presence. This encounter transformed him for the task ahead.

Moses also, went to the Mountain seeking direction, strength and a manifest face to face encounter with God. He became stubborn, waiting for more! But that tenacity paid off and he was strengthened, prepared and transformed for His destiny.

During times of decision, change of direction and hard battles do you go to the Mountain? OR Go it on your own and go to the Mattresses?

13

As in an old saying used by the mafia in Italy – "going to the mattresses" means you will stand your ground – fight for your cause with all you have, with no restraint. Going to the Mattresses says YOU can do it - <u>you go into this on your own strength, knowledge and ingenuity</u> (leaving the direction of the Holy Spirit out of the equation).

Here YOU do it all; it takes all of you and usually will drain you to below <u>empty.</u> This will bring you to a place of stress, frustration and pressure. All in all, it is a very nasty place for you and for those who are still standing around you.

You say, "Yeah, but I'm not Jesus or Moses" - true, but you have the same choice and access to the throne of God.

You can head to the Mountain! You can wait there (sometimes wait a long time) and allow the Holy Spirit to meet with you. He will pour out on you his peace, direction and encouragement; preparing you for the task ahead. He can prepare you up on that Mountain versus doing it yourself down on the Mattresses (where you really need a chance to stop and collapse when or if you make it out the other end).

You will still have the decisions and work to be done when you come down from the Mountain.

However, you have been prepared for the task and the approach and ultimate out-come is totally different.

My Choice is to Go To The Mountain!

He will overshadow me and give me a peace filled transformation for the coming journey.

Each time you encounter that cross roads you have the choice too.

Take a minute the next time and decide if you want to Go to the Mountain or Go to the Mattresses.

Philippians 4:6-7 - do not be anxious about anything, but in everything by prayer and supplication with thanksgiving let your requests be made known to God. And the peace of God, which surpasses all understanding, will guard your hearts and your minds in Christ Jesus.

The Seasons of Our Lives
A Different Way of Thinking
(Part 1 – Fall)

A recent read of a traditional thought regarding our lives and the seasons we go through caused my mind to do a double take and a new thinking began to emerge.

Our lives do mirror the seasons of nature, true - but I don't believe it is like we have thought. A cycle, yes - but a cycle that can be active and repeat in our lives sometimes daily, weekly, yearly and for varying time frames. The repetition of these cycles is part of life.

When we allow the flow of the seasons to have complete control we walk in a new understanding of what "being led by the Spirit" is really about. It's all about listening and moving from one season to the next when He speaks.

I love the Fall - so lets start there.

In nature it's a time of slowing down. Flowers have finished their spectacular display, trees have completed their fruiting purposes while squirrels and other gatherers are focused on one thing - preparation for the next season.

For us the Fall is a time of <u>simplification</u>, where we begin pulling all distractions away and focus becomes pinpoint - directed to His plan.

It's a time of preparation. This time can be for today's directed project or for an extended period as we wait for an appointed time of action.

This time of simplification requires you to make a choice. It is a choice to stop and pull away all the extra busyness you have accumulated. Prepare for His purpose and plan for your life by allowing empty time to exist.

It requires extensive time where you are content to sit at His feet and learn to rest and listen as He speaks.

Join me in this place of learning to simplify your life in preparation for His call.

The Seasons of Our Lives

A Different Way of Thinking

(Part 2 – Winter)

I look at winter differently too.

What's winter in nature? It's a quiet time, a time of active rest and peace.

Active rest because a lot happens in those quiet underground-unseen places of nature. During this quiet time strength is infused to all types of roots. It's a time of multiplication. Life is being conceived both in wildlife as well as bulbs and seeds. These are all examples of natures expected growth to come.

For us, I don't see it as a dark night of the soul or suffering that God puts us through. NO WAY! Not my Jesus!

During this time for us it's a time for wheels to stop turning. The "I can do" lays down to rest in what "He did".

It's a time for us to sit at His feet, gather strength, learn to wait and trust His plan for each day and for our life.

It's a time of expectant multiplication as we rest and wait. This can be an hour in our day or years - it's all about His timing.

18

The Seasons of Our Lives

A Different Way of Thinking

(Part 3 – Spring)

Spring emerges from winters rest and with it a new hope and an explosion of energy - creating new life for all of nature.

The trees bud, flowers bloom and babies are born.

As you feel, smell and hear spring approach something within your very being begins to stir. It's a promise of new life that is ignited by the very emergence of the small internal voice saying "Yes" and "Amen" to the Creators' promises.

You begin to have new directions, new visions, renewed hope, new strength and energy to drive forward that which you are hearing His voice proclaim over your life.

During this spring stirring take time to journal all the exciting thoughts, questions, directions and plans that He has been speaking into your spirit during winters rest. These will begin to bloom as you lay them at His feet and wait for His directions.

Rejoice in the assurance of His love and plans for you.

The Seasons of Our Lives
A Different Way of Thinking
(Part 4 - Summer)

Then comes summer; we all love summer! Nature and man alike can bask with all of our senses as creation vibrates with life.

Nature gets her opportunity to show off to us as she produces beautiful flowers, foliage, fruits and nuts. She orchestrates songs of rejoicing from wildlife. She energizes movement of waters as well as the radiating warmth of the sun. Fresh breezes that breathe through the trees and flowers are all part of her expression. All of our senses come alive as we partake in her offerings. Her amazing aromas, unspeakable displays of beauty, and warming sunrays seep deep into our lives. Her refreshing breezes and scrumptious flavors of fresh produce tantalize our senses.

For us summer brings times of great enjoyment.

Fruitfulness as His favor and abundant provision is poured out on all that we put our hand to.

This cycle can be enjoyed daily or as often as you are blessed with it.

The gift of summer truly is meant by God to be a gift to His children. He desires His kids to have fun and take time to lean back and relax.

He already paid for this vacation. It's an all expenses paid gift from His son Jesus. Just accept it and know that it's ok to enjoy summer and walk in life filled with continual refreshment.

Psalm 84:11-12 - For the Lord God is a sun and shield; the Lord bestows favor and honor. No good thing does he withhold from those who walk uprightly. O Lord of hosts, blessed is the one who trusts in you.

Psalm 13:5-6 - But I have trusted in your steadfast love; my heart shall rejoice in your salvation. I will sing to the LORD, because he has dealt bountifully with me.

Cinderella and the Bride of Christ

As children we fall in love with the fairy tales of Princesses and Princes. Little girls become women with the "Cinderella syndrome" buried in their hearts. Little boys become men looking to rescue their "one true love".

Why is that so deep within us?

I think that somewhere inside of all of us is the hope that there is truth in those stories. So, lets look at this differently for a moment.

Our prince, Jesus will come. He is waiting to return for His bride and to whisk her away to His magic kingdom with streets of gold and crystal waters for all eternity.

Cinderella was born into nobility yet was forced into servitude. She lived where evil prevailed daily and was treated as evil by her own family members. So happens to us - the Bride of Christ.

She IS noble but her true identity has been covered over with the thinking and distractions of this world. Buried like a charwoman who is covered with soot, grime and ash this once beautiful noble bride has lost sight of her one true love.

The Bible says that our prince is returning for a Bride that has made herself ready.

Just as Cinderella had a secret place that sustained her, a place of joy that welled up within her, a place that brought songs erupting from within and brought change to her heart; so must the Bride of Christ find that secret place where the face of Jesus is the <u>one thing</u> that matters. Then her identity will shine through, her hopelessness will begin to fall away and she will erupt with joy that will change the very atmosphere around her.

As with Cinderella, the favor will present itself and in an instant the change from scullery maid to Bride will occur. Her eyes will be only for her prince. All else will fade away. His return on a white horse to whisk her away to the magic kingdom is eminent.

Let's find that secret place and focus only on the face of our beloved. Let's be the Bride that has made herself ready. Let's have our hand on the door ready when our prince rides up on his white horse with glass slipper in hand. Let's rejoice in knowing that He has come for us!

Revelation 22:17 - The Spirit and the Bride say, "Come." And let the one who hears say, "Come." And let the one who is thirsty come; let the one who desires take the water of life without price.

Reflections of His Glory

Spring's Assurance

Reflections of His Glory

Winter's Thaw – "Some People Are Worth Melting For"

For generations fairy tales have captured our hearts; the hero's, princess's, prince's and villains but today a recent award-winning story is part of my contemplation. We can often find spiritual meaning in the natural as well as in our beloved fairy tales.

The thaw of winter begins deep within the frozen ground where seeds ready for germination rest and wait. The stirring within the seed begins and its purpose pulses – ready for eruption.

Just as the frozen winter ground accepts the suns caressing rays of warmth in order to begin that thaw; often we find ourselves frozen inside, waiting and needing some way to begin the thawing of our hearts.

We find ourselves frozen by fear. Who we are is trapped inside with no escape from the storms that rage continually within. Fear has become our only companion; causing anger, bitterness and condemnation to reign and our hearts become frozen and hard. We tell ourselves to "conceal, don't feel, don't show, don't let them in, don't let them see". We fear that who we are just isn't good enough.

The reality is that just as Olaf said "some people are worth melting for" and Anna sacrificed herself with an act of true love to unfreeze her sisters heart; we have a true sacrifice of love given for us at the cross of Christ.

If you "let it go" and accept one ray of His love you can say good-bye to your past.

Jesus provided one act of sacrificial love that will thaw your frozen heart and the "first time in forever" you will walk through an open door filled with love and acceptance for who you are. The past will not haunt you ever again, as you draw into the warmth of Christ. In the presence of His loving warmth the fear, condemnation, anger and bitterness will melt.

Spring will break forth over you. Who you are and all that you are capable of becoming will begin to erupt just as the warming seeds begin to germinate into the beauty that is encapsulated within them.

Step into His warmth, "let it go" and allow His love to melt the frozen parts of your heart.

The Fog Veil Was Torn

In nature we find veils of fog in many places. Today, two bring me to contemplate a comparison of nature versus spiritual.

A misty veil of fog slowly materializes on the earth causing a nearly silent enclosure. This can be life threatening if you happen to be the captain of a ship at sea.

A veil of fog also slowly materializes over our eyes as we age, causing cataracts that though not life threatening can destroy clarity of vision and disrupt life.

Just as that veil of fog settles over the land and a cloudy cataract enshrouds our eye, so can a clouding slip over our heart.

In the natural we have designed fog horns to loudly cut through the fog and signal those at sea the proximity of danger; thus giving them hope and safety.

A cataract is now removed during a swift surgery that cracks the offensive cloudy lens and places a new clear one, thus allowing a previously veiled eye to see with new clarity the world that was veiled.

Often we are living a life unaware of a fog that has drifted over our heart and eyes. We live a life filled with daily survival.

When we see Jesus for the 1st time, we hear the foghorns signal; hope and forgiveness rush in and safety is found. However, there is so much more. Distractions seem to catch us all unaware, just as the fog on the road or the cataract in our eye.

Jesus sacrifice tore the veil – the fog – between heaven and earth, pouring forth the very breath of God that is available to you. This breath is much more then forgiveness, it's a new life filled with ALL His promises and favor. <u>Jesus bought you a brand new life</u>.

He replaced the foggy lenses of your eyes with crystal clear ones that can see with newfound clarity. This brightness of vision is filled with the destiny that was given to you at your birth.

Due to distractions of life you find that fog has quietly taken over your once joy filled walk with Jesus; your vision has faded, and you are firmly embedded in this drifting fog bank. Much of your clarity and promise of destiny has been swallowed up.

Just as the removal of a cataract is a swift procedure so is the restoration of all that was given to you. His favor is always available and the removal of that fog can dissipate in an instant by looking up to the Son.

Remember the veil was torn for you!

Allow new birth and revelation of His love to erupt over your heart and eyes. It will bring renewal to what has been covered and an awakened stirring of new sight and direction. His plans and purposes for you will begin to be seen as clarity resurfaces.

Hebrews 4:16 - Let us then with confidence draw near to the throne of grace, that we may receive mercy and find grace to help in time of need.

Silencing the Voices of Winter

I find something astonishing about the tiny brilliant colored crocus flowers. They are designed to push up through the ground at a time when all of nature is still asleep. They feel a ray of warmth that most of nature misses and it stirs them to believe for what is true and close at hand.

They are sprinkled for weeks with dustings of snow, chilled by the frosty breath of winds and adorned with frost every morning but they still stand tall proclaiming their internal knowledge of the truth of the emanate arrival of spring.

The crocus's appearance signals within us as well - our knowing that even though the snow still lightly may fall, the wind still blows its chilly breath and the slippery icy frost still awaits our footprints in the morning - the warmth of spring is unfolding. These voices of winter are silenced because we believe in the creator's consistent design of nature.

Within each of us is that spiritual "knowing" of our design as well. Our life situations may not look different – the snows are still falling, the winds are still blowing and the frosty mornings still arrive – but inside is a promise that was fulfilled at the cross for each of us.

Just as the crocus raises its tiny head in colorful victory we too can stand strong in His promise. His promise of complete forgiveness is given as a gift and brings us the strength of the crocus to push back the voices that whisper of our past failures and faults.

His abundant extravagant love poured out doesn't remember any of them.

Look forward with me daily to walking as the crocus – full of expectation of spring's complete work within you.

Isaiah 54:10 - For the mountains may depart and the hills be removed, but my steadfast love shall not depart from you, and my covenant of peace shall not be removed," says the Lord, who has compassion on you.

Lamentations 3:22-23 - The steadfast love of the Lord never ceases; his mercies never come to an end; they are new every morning; great is your faithfulness.

Step Over the Threshold or Slam the Door

Just as the flowering trees of spring signal that spring is arriving; so do your life experiences create your personal life paradigm.

This life paradigm is one that says, "When I see this" - "this is the result".

Your need to "see it" to "believe it" isn't something new to society, it's the same innate thinking that Jesus saw as He taught the multitudes.

At the lake of Gennesaret after a long night of fishing, the natural in Peter questioned Jesus when He told him to let his nets down again for a catch. However, Peter chose to say, "Yes". His response allowed Jesus to perform a miracle that was witnessed by him and many others.

To the multitudes amazement they "saw it" – a catch so large that it took two boats to the brink of sinking. They knew this was not a natural experience.

To Peter it triggered a faith eruption, seeing beyond his life paradigm and it became a life-altering experience. He left what he knew and followed Jesus.

So my question has been, why did Jesus do that?

I believe He knew all the fears and accusations Peter would experience in years to come and Jesus gave Peter a "see it" to "believe it" moment to draw a line in the sand for him. Here was a moment in time for him to remember – a place to stand and push back the lies, fears and accusations that would come to whisper in his ear.

The plan for His life unfolded the day he chose to follow Jesus and leave his nets. However, the life he entered held many obstacles and the catch of fish that one eventful day opened his eyes to who Jesus was.

We all live with decisions made or not made, and with regrets that can whisper for years in our ears.

The silencing of those lies, accusations and fears was done for us at the cross of Jesus. If we make the choice to look only at the face of Jesus and His poured out love that was given to us undeserved; then we can stand victorious against those lies, fears and accusations, and move into the great plans and purposes that we are designed for.

We too, experience by the Holy Spirits direction things that defy our life paradigm and we too, must make a choice to step over the threshold and through that door believing or slam the door in disbelief.

These decisions can be life-altering experiences for us.

They can lead us to see who Jesus is and bring us to a fulfilling purpose or they can keep us in a life that lives continually in the "see it" to "believe it" cycle of existence.

My choice is to walk in a new paradigm, one that is God designed – "He promised it so I believe it".

Hebrews 11:1 - Now faith is the assurance of things hoped for, the conviction of things not seen.

Creations Explosion of
New Life and Promise!

As we feel, smell and hear spring approaching it stirs and renews something inside of our very being. It's a promise of new life that is ignited by the very emergence of the small internal voice saying "YES" and "Amen" to the creators promise.

There is a perpetual movement within nature that precedes spring.

Weeks before, temperatures begin to warm. The signaling begins the onset of spring and something begins to stir in all of creation. It's a belief, a faith that has been placed deep inside of her. That faith is that New Life is possible and is coming.

With that begins a stirring and a movement that grows within the very sap of the trees, the hull of the seeds, the growing creation within the eggs and the wombs of the unborn animals; it is the YES and AMEN of creation to the creators promise of new life.

Once the time has come - the eruption begins its song as the buds of trees and flowers burst into bloom. Seeds dormant under the earth now explode into life while birds of all species and sizes begin the process of their hatching. They begin the pecking and cracking open of their protective shell, and the birthing process of animals all around us begins to burst forth with the sounds of new life.

All of nature sings forth with conformation of that internal voice of faith in His promises.

We too, with anticipation of spring's creative explosion see promise and new life around our lives.

His plan is always for you!   His plan is for promise and new life in your family, your job, your physical being etc.

Join me today as we say YES and AMEN to His promises for our lives.

II Corinthians 1:20 – For all the promises of God find their Yes in him. That is why it is through him that we utter our Amen to God for his glory.

Ready to Run Before the Wind

As a sailboat with an unbalanced load will list and drift off its course, often a similar drifting time can occur in your life.

Questions, pain and loneliness begin to flow in and out. Faith anchors you to a deep stillness and contentment within that ultimately will prevail.

Staying the storm, waiting for the wind to stir and purposefully setting about trimming and rebalancing the load takes a dependence on the knowledge of His plans and purposes for your life.

Your faith and understanding of who you are as an heir in the Kingdom is your strength and anchor.

Timing in the process is crucial. A turn in direction made to quickly will cause disaster, ending in pulling you out of the wind and the ultimate possibility of capsize or luffing - no wind in the sails or desire for it.

The Lord keeps you in a safe harbor - keeping you safe from all attack as time and preparation work within you. As you rest in this safe harbor the turning process begins.

This place of preparation allows you to trim your sails, adjusting them to allow maximum efficiency as the sails become "Full".

The fullness of your sails will bring you to a healthy place of "getting on with the job" that He has placed before you.

This fullness will allow this job it to be done in a steady relaxed way, without stress and urgency.

Just as a sailboat begins to "come about", the turning begins ever so slightly as each wave is taking you toward a new direction, allowing momentum to carry you forward.

This time of turning is often a lonely difficult place. However, it will direct you into an awareness that will slowly surge within and stir anticipation for the coming process. At the appropriate time you will begin to cry out for what is to come.

You will come to a new place where with sails trimmed and full you will be propelled forward into new waters - ready to run before the wind.

The adventure ahead will be one of full sails, movement and new horizons. You will see new places in the spirit and be moved to heights of effectiveness that you have never imagined.

As the stillness begins to change, you can feel the beginning of a breeze. With a breath that quivers within and the surge of movement – the rise of a wave begins to break.

"It is time, it is time, it is time!
Catch it now!
Run before the wind!"

The waves begin to respond to the breeze as they rise and fall. The sails begin to breath in and out just as your spirit begins to anticipate the coming movement.

Don't hold back.

Feel the freedom that comes with the movement. Step into the call He has placed within you.

Now is the time to sail forward being propelled into all that He has purposed and prepared for you.

You are ready to run before the wind.

Psalm 17:5-8 - My steps have held fast to your paths; my feet have not slipped. I call upon you, for you will answer me, O God; incline your ear to me; hear my words. Wondrously show your steadfast love, O Savior of those who seek refuge from their adversaries at your right hand. Keep me as the apple of your eye; hide me in the shadow of your wings,

---

Psalm 37:23-24 - The steps of a man are established by the Lord, when he delights in his way; though he fall, he shall not be cast headlong, for the Lord upholds his hand.

Psalm 91:1-2 - He who dwells in the shelter of the Most High will abide in the shadow of the Almighty. I will say to the Lord, "My refuge and my fortress, my God, in whom I trust."

Note: (To help those of us who are not nautical in our understanding the following are for better clarity of the above prose.)
My understanding of the following sailing terms:

"Full" sails = getting on with the job but in a steady relaxed way, without undue urgency or strain.

Listing = leaning and drifting

Trimming the sails = adjustment needed to improve balance and bring maximum efficiency.

Unbalanced load = Is a defect needing correction

Tacking / heeling = changing direction

Coming about = the momentum that carries the vessel forward.

Luffing= no wind in the sail

Running downwind (Running before the wind) = wind directly behind you moving you forward.

The Beauty of First Flight – Believe You Are Made For More!

The butterfly's journey begins long before her first flight. Starting with the caterpillar that doesn't comprehend that a transformation waits ahead. Its hunger pushes it forward foraging for life-giving sustenance that will allow the strength for the formation of a freshly spun place of private metamorphosis. Upon arrival in this cocoon the process begins. It is the time to rest, to wait, to trust in the creators plan. The transformation that transpires while sealed in this cocoon is remarkable. It allows a creation that was made to crawl find its wings to fly. Soon the cocoon opens and releases this new beauty. She comes forth - unfurls her wings and RESTS in the SUN, here waiting for the strength to lift her new found wings and take her first flight.

Finally anticipation swells within and as gentle as a breath she lifts up upon those paper thin wings and launches into a new life that now involves new heights and new horizons that could never have been achieved without this transformation.

The willingness to *"Be Still and Know that I Am God"* is that process of metamorphosis that allows the caterpillar to become the butterfly.

It will also allow a transformation in your life that will take you from one who strives to one who trusts completely in your Lord.

The thought process of "<u>work to **achieve** all that there is to success</u>" is exchanged for one that "**<u>believes</u>** <u>you are made for more</u>".

You can REST in the SON for His release, His direction and His wind of abundance that will be blown beneath newfound wings that are ready to launch into a life that involves new heights and new visions.

Your anticipation will swell inside as the wind and the spirit come beneath your wings to carry you higher and further then you could have gone by your own work as the caterpillar.

Believe you are made for more and take that first flight of "Being Still and Knowing that He is God"!

Psalm 46:10 - "Be still, and know that I am God. I will be exalted among the nations, I will be exalted in the earth!"

Be Who You Were Created To Be

A well-known slogan often rings in our ears, "Be all you can be", but we were created to be exactly who we are. We already are all we can be if we acknowledge and walk in that assurance.

The Fathers original design in nature expresses itself to us again in the simple concept of being who you were created to BE. Nature knows that which it is created to be and it just IS!

Grapes grow grapes; even when grafted, they still produce grapes not flowers. An apple tree knows within its design what it is to produce; trying to produce an orange just won't work. Birds, Fish and animals all pro—create from their own kind. They just know instinctively who they are and it's easy; it's natural and peace reigns. No working, researching, studying required; they KNOW how to BE!

We humans on the other hand try so hard to BE better, BE happier, BE different, or BE someone else.

If we can learn to rest and BE at peace with who we are and what we were created to BE, our purpose will present itself and will bring us fulfillment and peace. Fruit will be automatic; we will just Be!

Many times we may require 40 years in the wilderness of TRY, TRY, TRY before we come to a place where we can stop, look around and see what it means to just BE!

The key we must find is GOD; not rules, regulations, TO DO's and DO NOT's but meeting HIM face to face. HIS presence brings that understanding and will change you.

Living in the place of HIS presence, hearing HIS voice and tapping into the chemistry within makes you WHO you are. Knowing who you are will bring a freedom of knowing how to BE.

That freedom will reveal the chemistry that ONLY you were designed with. ONLY your unique thoughts, abilities, gifts, and personality where made with HIS purpose in mind. Your very DNA - unique ONLY to you can produce the specific fruit that HE planned. NO trying is involved. Just BE and walk in that confidence that YOU already are ALL YOU can BE.

Life Giving Presence – The River

The parallels of nature and spiritual intrigue me as I contemplate our lives and our need for strength, support and relationships that often come from connecting with a body of people who believe as we do. The church, with all her faults just happens to be that body.

Just as a drop of water that is entombed in a dark cloud anticipates release into the small beckoning spring below, so are we. This raindrops release unites it with the refreshing spring as it becomes one with the forming "rivlets". These flow in turn in a steady motion forward marching toward the stream of living water that is bubbling and greeting them from below.

As they merge into this stream they grow in strength and speed seeking out and forming ways to reach the next goal of uniting with a wider, deeper and more forceful body called The River.

The River has an identity of its own! Joining with this body the anticipation grows overwhelming. The purpose as part of this river will be to bring life to all that grows on its banks and to all that inhabits its depths. The speed, force, depth and width of this amazing river changes as each stream enters.

The river creates its own path even breaking into new areas and over barriers of rock allowing the formation of cascading falls that refresh previously barren and dry land. This Rivers very existence draws creation to its banks for the life giving presence it provides. This water brings refreshment and life, strengthening all that lives within its presence, changing the very atmosphere.

As nature parallels the spiritual so are we as that drop of water. Once we find The River – a body of believers - that brings life to us, so sets our purpose.

Seek the presence and face of Jesus that will give you strength and life and a River where you can grow and be part of changing the very atmosphere around you.

Psalm 42:1 - As a deer pants for flowing streams, so pants my soul for you, O God.

Mission - Possible

"Your mission if you choose to accept it". These words you all know from popular entertainment but let's consider them in a spiritual sense.

You make a choice to step into many activities in your life. Whether it is at church, work or in extracurricular activities, you find yourself in the impossible situation of "fitting".

How you act, speak and relate to people in those arenas are all connected to that "fitting" process.

Many of them are necessary and many are chosen; but when you honestly evaluate this process you may find it is just plain hard work. What in reality you are doing is trying to fit a round peg into a square hole; it's just not possible.

But "fitting" isn't what you as the "Bride of Christ" are asked to do. In fact it is the exact opposite. Your face and focus needs to be totally on the face of Christ.

You are different and are as a single flower amidst the shrubs. The "fitting" mentality is all about "us" not "Him". The "Him" assignment (mission) focus means that He directs your decisions and your involvement in all areas of your life.

It means your current road will become narrow, directed and more fulfilling because He knows the plans and purposes that your life was designed for.

He has the place that is exactly designed for his single flower to be placed.

The "Him" focus turns your eyes off of your "fitting". You stop and simply ask, "What is my assignment (my mission)?

That assignment can be for an hour, a day, a year or a lifetime. Your part is to ask, choose to accept it and do it. It's not going to be about you but what He has chosen for you to do and in it you will find pure joy.

Living your life in this manner means accepting those assignments whether you "think" you can accomplish them or not.

His assignments often seem impossible to you; but when He gives you a "mission impossible" assignment then you can believe that <u>He will make it possible</u>.

Join me to lay down the "fitting" process. Step out and allow your road to become narrow. Accept the impossible assignments that the Holy Spirit is stirring inside of you and let Him make the impossible possible.

No Worries – Just Sing

Watching the multitude of different birds that converge on my yard for their daily dance and song, I can't help but smile. Their symphony of different sounds begins with the sun and erupts as they fly in, take their quick turn at the feeders and move over for the next species.

They have no concern that it won't be there or won't be enough. They trust their provider to meet their daily needs.

No worries…just singing.

As the current seed provider, a smile and joy swell in my soul, causing me to ponder this sight. I can't help but wonder how our heavenly Father, our provider, must smile when He sees our trust.

His heart must swell with love as the understanding of His love for us, provision and constant attention to every detail in our lives, begins to register in our hearts. What a joy and smile we must bring to Him.

I can only imagine how He must feel when He sees us enjoying and trusting in His provisions with joy in our hearts and a song on our lips. I can almost hear Him say, "No Worries….Just Sing".

Encouragement Brings New Life

Words of affirmation and encouragement are building blocks to every heart.

The words we speak to those around us can cut down or build up. Those words once spoken can never be taken back. So our choice daily is - which do we want to speak, words that build or words that hurt?

We can daily make choices to walk, leaning on and listening to the voice of the Holy Spirit and become true encouragers or allow our own words to gush forth in a tidal wave of emotion that usually will bring forth destruction.

I desire my words to heal, lift, bring a smile and change a life. Listening and speaking His words will bring life because true encouragement is the heart of the Father. If we make a choice to walk as an encourager we can bring His heart to our world.

Philippians 2:1-4 - So if there is any encouragement in Christ, any comfort from love, any participation in the Spirit, any affection and sympathy, complete my joy by being of the same mind, having the same love, being in full accord and of one mind. Do nothing from selfish ambition or conceit, but in humility count others more significant than yourselves. Let each of you look not only to his own interests, but also to the interests of others.

"With This Ring"

"With this ring…." Is a phrase every couple repeats as they make a marriage commitment to each other. The meaning of those three little words has impact and significance that we rarely consider.

An intended bride waits in breathless anticipation for her beloved to extend his intent to make her his bride when he presents that sparkling ring.

He has willingly chosen to lay down his own life and give all he has for this one. His eyes and face shine with great joy and anticipation of the presentation and acceptance of this shining circle given as a token of all the love that he has exploding from within. Placing it on her finger signals her acceptance and desire to commit her life completely to him. Her eyes overflow with love and trust. Her glowing smile and giddy joy show no doubt in his acceptance of who she is.

The understood meanings of commitment, trust, love, and honor are all part of the acceptance of this shining symbol. However, these meanings we tend to ignore in our society. They are present nonetheless. Those meanings are the bride's acceptance of a new name as well as the power and authority that her new name and position hold.

We see the rich and famous signing prenuptial agreements in order to keep their own "things" to themselves – just in case.

Our groom; Jesus pours out lavishly upon his bride and ALL that is His belongs to us.

We, as the bride of Christ have also received this presentation of our bridegroom's signet ring. Thus acknowledging his eternal commitment, his poured out love and unconditional acceptance for us, his bride. We also have been given a new name that includes his power and authority.

Our understanding and use of what that means is rather overwhelming; but if we can receive this revelation our lives will be transformed as we walk in that given favor, power and authority that the name of Jesus Christ bought for us.

Our new name has already been proclaimed in heaven and that ring gives us HIS name and with that comes His power and authority. Everything that belongs to him belongs to us.

Let's accept and place that ring with all its authority upon our finger and move into the places He has called us to tread.

I Peter 2:9 - But you are a chosen race, a royal priesthood, a holy nation, a people for his own possession, that you may proclaim the excellencies of him who called you out of darkness into his marvelous light.

Summer's Delight

Reflections of His Glory

The Beauty of a Bleeding Heart

There is a strikingly beautiful plant hidden in many gardens that intrigues me. The comparison of its name – "Bleeding Heart" to its visual grace appears to be an oxymoron.

She is stirred to awaken as soon as warming temperatures arrive. Quietly with no great fanfare her arrival begins as thin green shoots of soft foliage begin to emerge. Then with incredible grace an arching spray of dainty dripping heart shaped flowers cascade out of the center of the soft green mound. Appearing almost over night. Each of these tiny flowers resemble a perfect heart with a tiny drop of color coming from the tip, thus acquiring the name "bleeding heart".

Comparing this plant to your spiritual life is two fold, your heart and the heart of Christ.

The thought of a "bleeding heart" is one of pain. Hearts are broken, hurt and desensitized by hurts inflicted by others, by natural circumstances and by wrong decisions. However, the poured out life of Jesus shows a different kind of "bleeding heart".

His love for you was so great. He exchanged his life for yours. This exchange gives you eternal life and a new heart. His heart was a "bleeding heart" of grace and mercy as His blood was poured out just for you.

When you can take your "bleeding heart" and through the cross of Christ give that pain to him, receiving his forgiveness - then your heart is open to finding His love and acceptance. The once "bleeding heart" in you is changed and becomes a thing of beauty. Your heart then is allowed to become just like the graceful beauty of the "bleeding heart" plant in my garden – free to be the beauty that is hidden within.

Let your "bleeding heart" be changed by giving it to Jesus. His love changes it into a transformed creation. Your choice is to accept His gift and allow the process to begin.

No Weeds, No Fences in the Kingdom

I love to meander and enjoy a beautifully manicured flower garden – no fences, no weeds, no encroaching grass and no invasion of space by another species. Unfortunately those gardens don't exist in most neighborhoods unless there is a full time gardener employed.

Just as a well cared for garden allows for both beauty and fragrance to meld together for an unimaginable aroma - each of you are filled with treasures of different types – gifts that have been given to you. Your specific type and fragrance is different from the one next to you and it is only made better by their presence alongside.

When you walk in the Kingdom of God with your eyes focused on Christ - your individual aroma can be enjoyed and the very fragrance within permeates your atmosphere.

However, often you will find yourself trying to smell or look just like the one next to you or assume they are in your way and begin pushing them out. Your own needs for acceptance, validation and affirmation begin to change the look that your gardener had planned for this garden. Fences begin to divide up the landscape; weeds, encroaching grass and invasion of space change the garden from His intended plan.

Thankfully, you have a loving full time gardener who can adjust those unwanted weeds, encroaching grass and unnecessary invasion of space by lovingly showing you who you are in Him. Your significance and purpose can be trusted into His hands.

If your focus is always on Christ – He will quickly redirect any unwanted change to His landscape in your life.

With a full time gardener on your side your individual aroma can be enjoyed and the fragrance within will merge with those around you. You then begin to saturate your atmosphere with a scent of completeness that only comes from many single focused scents becoming one.

Your Christ focus will eliminate the encroaching grass and all weeds. There will be no need for fences for this garden will have no boundaries. Its beauty will be as astounding as your individual varieties. For now, as each of you with a singular scent produce exactly what and where the gardener planned. Honor for and encouragement of the species on your right and on your left only enhances this garden. For only when it melds into one is its true purpose seen.

Join me as you allow your scent to rejoice in a single Christ centered focus. Allow Him access to pull all weeds, all grass and pull down all fences.

Let's walk in a Kingdom side by side that has no weeds, no fences or self focused distractions.

Blooming In His Love

Great anticipation is stirred within me as I walk in my garden and watch the flower buds beginning to swell. Their individuality silently waiting to erupt into the hidden beauty they were created to be.

The understanding of the love of Christ within you is like the promise hidden within the budding flower – a transformation waits.

Waiting as the fullness of time passes - these buds will reveal an explosion of color, texture and scent as each one comes into its own fullness of beauty. This is shown off in a spectacular array as each specific flower exhibits its own created characteristic. Even when they are the same flower, side by side – they show off differences and individuality in their colors and shapes.

You too are similar in comparison. Your budding life in Christ comes into full bloom as you enter into the place of knowing the love and true identity that you carry as a child of the King. Only then can you come into full bloom and show forth the beauty of who you were created to be.

The process from bud to full bloom can't be rushed without damage or destruction to the flower.

Children love to pick a flower bud and then one petal at a time peel it apart. They are hoping to see the treasure that is hidden in the center.

Disappointment and frustration show on their little faces as they find only a hand-full of shriveling petals once the center is unveiled. They do not realize that the delight in its beauty is only found when time has completed its work.

So relax, rest in His presence, be content in the journey. Allow the truth of His love and acceptance to begin the process. As you "bloom in His love" the revelations of treasures hidden within you will soon burst into full bloom.

II Corinthians 4:7 - But we have this treasure in jars of clay, to show that the surpassing power belongs to God and not to us.

The Growth Process of a Seed

With excitement we prepare our gardens and plant seeds with anticipation of the end result. Consideration of the required process that the seed must take from beginning to end is not given much thought. However, let's consider that today.

We place each individual seed into the soil. Each one is given equal nutrition, water and sun. The seed does nothing. Slowly – over the appropriate time – it begins to germinate. Still – to our eyes - the seed is doing nothing, the process is just occurring.

Then like an eruption from within – it sprouts new life that pushes up through the soil. But the seed did nothing but WAIT. The life and the harvest come from within at just the right time.

Now what if the gardener became impatient and came back every day, pulling back the soil to check if the seed had grown yet. Or he may think that extra water or more fertilizer will make it grow faster. However, these excesses will only cause death or unproductive seeds – the planned harvest within the seed is destroyed.

Patience – waiting – trusting in the pre-planned purpose of that seed is the gardeners' hardest chore.

Each seed has a harvest quota programmed into its DNA – some 30, some 60 and some 100 fold.

We behave like the anxious gardener when we actually are the seed.

We find ourselves running here and there for better and more teaching, or working harder to achieve a place in the Kingdom. These activities are like adding excess water or fertilizer to the seed and often it results in stunted or destroyed seed.

Our place – as the seed - is to rest and wait. Trusting that where we have been placed is a nutrient rich well-watered soil. It will bring forth that which is within as it is consistently shined upon with His warmth. Our Heavenly Father has a planned harvest that He has placed within each of us – 30, 60 or 100 fold. It is not up to the seed to make it happen.

The DNA of whom and what we are to produce will be ignited and will erupt from within, bringing forth a fruitful harvest filled with completeness. No extra fertilizer required. Be patient and wait for the treasures placed within you to come forth.

As you focus on the face of Jesus – His love and rest will bring contentment to the destiny that is placed within you. His revelation and direction will be made clear. Freedom and refreshment will be your very heartbeat as your seed produces exactly what it is destined for.

Summers Stirring of Our Senses
The Gift of Sight

The fullness of summer expresses itself as it erupts around us. All five of our human senses are bombarded with the treasure-trove of experiences that come into the atmosphere as this extravagant season boldly fulfills its time.

We experience summer through sight, sound, taste, touch and smell as each sense is stirred within us.

We each find delight in summers abundance according to our own personal past and current circumstances. However, let's look at summer's expressions that we physically experience through our senses. Let's begin to compare our sensory experiences with the promises of Christ's contentment in our lives.

Through the visual gift of sight we experience the vivid explosion of color as flowers change places like colorful dancers on a dance floor.

Summer brings to our vision bluer skies, fluffier clouds and clearer star filled nights. Our sight is refreshed at the visual expression of cool waters as they splash over river rocks and crash as waves upon the warm sandy shores.

So many sights of peace come into our vision during summers outpouring of abundance. Most of them bring deep warmth – a center of contentment - to us physically, emotionally, mentally and spiritually.

God revelations – communications - come through a sight process. That sight can be an actual vision but most likely it's sight awareness from within. That awareness brings refreshing and peace.

With a single focus on Christ you will become visually attuned to life transforming understanding – internal sight – of who He is, what He did for you at the cross, and His love for you.

His gifts of refreshing and peace come from a hand filled with abundant love for you His child.

Allowing His reign and rule in your life, trusting that He always "has your back" will bring contentment in your journey. Enjoy a summer filled with eyes only for the face of your beloved.

Summers Stirring of Our Senses
The Gift of Sound

Our senses play a large part in how we experience things in our lives. Summer explodes with sounds that create lasting life memories. As spring moves into summer the sound of chirping birds and buzzing bees, as well as the scurry of rabbits and squirrels begins to stir anticipation of new life as summer explodes on the scene.

As we listen we hear the contagious joyous laughter of children, the clicking metallic sound of a sprinkler that delivers life-giving water to grass and seedlings, as well as the gurgle of streams and the crash of waves.

These sounds are only enjoyed if we listen and respond. If the busy activity of life overtakes our thoughts we can easily miss the enjoyment of these amazing gifts of summer.

Sound can come in thunderous explosions or in the slightest whisper. One is heard and felt – easily not missed. The other – is missed by most.

Tuning your spiritual ears to hear the very whisper of your Lord requires a deep place of contentment to rise within. This contentment comes as you willingly choose to listen.

As you surrender your busyness in exchange for His plans, step into a life that He directs and humbly consistently go to Him with a cry of "less of me and more of you" the listening process unfolds. These decisions will allow you to begin a journey of His destiny – one that will contentedly produce a courageous life full of faith.

Listening and responding in your spiritual life is often missed or lost because of distractions. Taking time to stop and listen to what the Holy Spirit speaks to you through the direction of Christ - requires a time where you stop and sit at the feet of Jesus.

Choose today the ONE THING that is important – to sit at the feet of your Lord. Then you will truly enjoy the gift of sound – hearing Him call your name!

Summers Stirring of Our Senses
The Gift of Taste

When you think of summer's abundance how can you help but find your mouth salivating.

Our senses are stirred at the thought of juicy dripping watermelon, fresh corn on the cob covered with warm butter, a red ripe strawberry bursting with sweetness along with many other amazing flavors found only in summer.

Our sense of taste is another gift that correlates with the abundance of Christ's promises that have been provided to us.

To taste in the natural requires us to reach out and take something into us. It's a choice we have to make. Sight and sound occur around us; however taste is one of our choice senses.

In the spiritual, God has also given us the choice to taste and see His goodness.

To enjoy foods placed before us "to nibble" vs "digging in" are two completely different things.

When we nibble on something it is just a little bite, usually because we are not sure if we will like it or not. When we dig in with no hesitation it is because we know what is placed before us is filled with amazing goodness.

Spiritually we often nibble for many reasons – fear being the biggest. Jesus and the Holy Spirit both came to show the goodness of God, His love for you and His promise that He will never leave you. Fear of anything is not in the equation. His love for you BREAKS off all fear.

If you are a "nibbler" in the spiritual chose today to believe that what He has for you is a plate filled with amazing goodness. Join me as we "dig in" and enjoy all of what He has for us. Taste and see just how good He is.

Summers Stirring of Our Senses
The Gift of Touch

The touch of contentment that we find in summer is as subtle as a breath of warm fresh air. It brings with it the warmth of sunrays and breezes that caress and cool. These touches wrap around us almost without our knowledge that they are present.

The touch of soft green grass on bare feet, a dive into a cool refreshing pool of water and a barefoot walk on a sandy shore are experiences of summer that we can again choose to enjoy or allow ourselves to pass up for lack of time or desire to experience them.

Summer brings an assortment of wonderful life filling experiences. The big decision often presents itself along with a personal question: "What do I give myself and time to in order to enjoy my summer this year?" We then chase after that which we have decided is the best fit.

The sense of touch is a very personal one to all of us. A physical touch signifies many things. It can be a touch of affection, one of encouragement, of greeting, or of joy. There are also many that bring pain – ones of rejection and anger – a push, a slap or a punch. Many of these – good and bad - we have experienced during our lives.

In a life that is filled with conflict and struggle our need for positive physical touch often causes us to look to others.

In our physical or emotional seeking for acceptance, affirmation and validation - physical touch pushes us into a "needy" place. This place pulls us away from the plans and purposes that Christ has for our lives. Our focus becomes similar to our deciding on what summer activities we want to enjoy. We are then looking and deciding according to what we think feels like a fit – or one of chasing after our needs - not one that is content in who we are in Christ.

His touch is what we truly crave for complete understanding of who we are in Him. All of our acceptance, affirmation and validation needs disappear as our focus is removed from US and placed on HIM.

The touch of the Holy Spirits presence has been given to you as a gift from Jesus and is a continual revelation of the Father's desire to walk among and with you in your life journey. This promise belongs to everyone who believes and it is His great delight to pour into you like a breeze that it is always available to cool and caress. His touch, His acceptance, His affirmation, His validation is ALL you need now and for eternity. His touch brings you to the feet of Jesus and brings your focus to being one that is all about the Lordship of Christ and bringing glory to Him.

Keeping your focus on the face of Jesus brings you complete freedom and contentment just as the warm fresh breeze that wraps around you in summer time.

Join me and bask in the touch of the Fathers hand, feel the caress of the Holy Spirits breeze and the intimate kiss of Lord Jesus.

Summers Stirring of Our Senses
The Gift of Smell

Smell is one of our senses that can trigger more memories in our lives than any others. Summers plethora of smells range from sweet flowers, fresh cut grass, grilling meat, burning campfires and salty waters to wet dogs and rotting vegetables.

How we respond to a scent will program it into our memories. Sweet flowers and fresh cut grass are distinct aromas – to the allergy sufferer they are to be avoided – to others enjoyed. The same goes for all smells – except maybe the rotting vegetables – which should be avoided at all costs.

In the spiritual, our very presence to those around us has an aroma. It can draw people to us or chase them away.

Is your smell one of enjoyment or one of rot?

Your life in Christ can be one that is like Mary who desired the ONE THING – to sit at the feet of Jesus or one like Martha that is busy about the "to do's" and represents judgment and law to those who don't believe. The scent that is expelled from you to those around you is an aroma of life or death.

Your love for Christ and those around you is a scent that is irresistible. Keeping your eyes on the face of Jesus will cause a contagious love to bubble out of your heart and along with that will be the expression of a scent of life.

Chose today to sit at the feet of Jesus. Focus on His face, allowing your love and contentment to rise to a level that only His love can accomplish in your life. His love will permeate your life and overflow to those around you. Your aroma will be one of love that will ignite memories of joy and love in the very atmosphere you live in - drawing others to find out what makes you smile. Then your joy will be made complete as you express His life and love to others.

Join me as we find contentment and delight in His presence. His aroma is the only scent my heart cries out for to carry within my being.

Transformation Awaits
Just Jump!

As the heat of summer begins its sizzle around us we look to the water to find the refreshing balance that our lives need. The shores of rivers begin to team with all ages of individuals looking for a way to delight themselves in its refreshment. The very presence of the cool river changes the atmosphere – internally and externally.

Just to sit on the edge of the river brings a semblance of coolness as its spray and breeze waft across our skin. Even our eyes seem to relax as we gaze at its movement.

Those who find the greatest pleasure at the rivers presence are those who in utter abandonment just jump into its waiting arms. They are completely immersed in its cool wet saturation. The joy that they experience is obvious. They emerge refreshed and transformed.

A hot, cranky, tired person is changed in a splash to a refreshed, exhilarated and joy-filled one.

As our lives bring us to a place of "over heated", finding the refreshment of a spiritual transformation also can be easily found if we run to the source.

Our source of refreshment and completeness is found at the river. Jesus is our source – our river. He promises us His presence and with that the Holy Spirit is available to bring transformation and comfort.

Our choices are to sit on the side of the river and receive a light breeze or occasional splash or we too can just jump in – overwhelmed by delight.

My choice is to just jump!

Total abandonment – immersed over my head – plunged into the depths!

The result is always immerging transformed, exhilarated refreshed and filled with joy.

Join me – Let's just jump!

Psalms 36:5-9 - Your steadfast love, O Lord, extends to the heavens, your faithfulness to the clouds. Your righteousness is like the mountains of God; your judgments are like the great deep; man and beast you save, O Lord. How precious is your steadfast love, O God! The children of mankind take refuge in the shadow of your wings. They feast on the abundance of your house, and you give them drink from the river of your delights. For with you is the fountain of life; in your light do we see light.

Hesitant, Confident or "Sold-Out" Jumper?

As I observe the rivers activity on a hot sunny day I can't help but smile as I watch people prepare to jump into the river.

The long wooden dock extending out over the river allows for many to line up and jump into the waiting cool depths.

Everyone is dressed and ready for water play but you find many different approaches to accomplish the planned activity.

There are those who are hesitant, those who appear confident and those who are enthusiastic – coming with total abandonment as they approach.

Each of these three groups has different ways to actually obtain the result. No discrimination of age or sex, each of them plans on getting into the waiting arms of the refreshing water but how they achieve it is totally individualized.

First – the hesitant ones. They all look down and evaluate the water below; but then this group seems to find different ways to reach the goal. Sit and slide over the edge, stoop down and with a slight jump - land with a splash. Lastly those who seem somewhat braver - get right to the edge and jump straight off submerging with a slight cutting splash.

Now – <u>the confident appearing ones</u>. They also stop and look at the water below them but with less concern. They have decided that they are getting in and there is a very slight hesitation. But here too you find different jumping techniques. This group usually backs up and makes a running jump – some feet first, some "cannon ball" style, some with a bended knee dive. This group always reaches the water with a thunderous splash and is very aware that others are watching.

Then come <u>the utterly "sold out" enthusiastic jumpers</u>. This group knows the water is there and waiting so there is no need to step to the edge and look down. They don't notice or care about any on-lookers and they seem to jump according to some automatic instinct. They still have different styles of jumping – those who run and jump, those who "cannon ball, those who "belly flop" and those who cut the water with a deep knee dive. However, their goal is only focused on getting into the river and enjoying all the delight and refreshment it has to offer.

We will find ourselves in one of these three groups. As we compare these groups of jumpers to our own spiritual desire for all the delightful refreshment that is available to us through Christ, our style will become evident. These groups and each jumper's style will change over our spiritual lives.

Trusting Jesus in every detail of our lives will ultimately bring us to a place where we no longer need to look down to see if He - the water - is there.

We will know we are safe and the concern to be noticed as we jump will no longer direct our lives.

We will come with total abandonment and jump into the very presence of Jesus with trust in His complete fullness for our life.

How we jump differs – we are all different in our style of enjoyment of His presence – let go and just jump!

Trusting Him with all the details of your life leads to a life of full surrender. It will bring a contentment that will allow you freedom to walk into the center of the river and all that He has planned for your life.

Keep jumping until your depth of trust brings you to the center of His presence and the greatest depths and refreshment in Christ – total Lordship.

Float the Center of the River

The delight in summer's warmth brings us back to the comforting relief found in the cool waters of a tranquil river.

Along the banks are boisterous games being played, children running and laughing, barbeques crackling and emitting their inviting scents along with those whose feet and legs are engulfed in the refreshing dip of "just a little" water.

All of these activities bring joy and delight but looking to the center of the river you will find a lone rubber raft floating and rolling along with the current.

My desire draws me to that singular place. There in the center of the river the water is the deepest and most refreshing. There it flows with a pure clarity. In that place you find quietness; all activity on the rivers edge melts away and is silenced. The current in the center is in total control – freely flowing.

In Christ – our center of the river –we find the deepest water, purity and complete refreshment. There is peace and rest in that center as our control is given up and His face is our focus.

His love for us is deep and wide and He beckons for our presence to come and join Him.

When we decide to step into the river our control is laid down. As we place our focus upon the source of our fulfillment – Jesus – then we are free to flow with the rivers current.

Our plans and purposes become nil as we allow the current to take us deeper into the center. Soon where the current goes we will find freedom as we float where it leads.

All thoughts of "our" plans float away. Delight in His presence brings clarity to our purpose. It is ALL about HIM. HE is our center and with that understanding comes a deep contentment to enjoy the float in the center of the river.

Join me in the safest, most refreshing river raft run of your life – one that is totally out of your control.

We Are His Chosen Stones

As the sun begins to rise over the still surface of the lake, not a single ripple stirs. The quiet morning allows for the beckoning opportunity of skipping a stone across its glassy surface. The desire wins and the stones are carefully chosen.

As one stone after another is strategically thrown, a cascade of movement begins to shimmer. In ripples it begins its expansive advancement across the width of the lake. Each stone bounces several times before finding its final silent descent. The once still surface now coming alive with ripples in all directions reaching to the distant shore.

Watching the change that a few chosen stones can make draws my mind to contemplate our lives as those chosen stones – strategically cast upon His waters – our world, our country, our community, our family.

As chosen stones in our Lords hand we have been strategically released into the atmosphere that surrounds our daily lives.

As a stone resting in His hand we are ready to be released. We silently wait for the movement and ripple effect that our very presence will bring. That effect depends not on the stones presence but the pitchers determination and original intent. His desire is the catalyst.

Some skipping stones skip once, some twice and some multiple times – again determined only by the pitchers intent.

As our pitcher releases us - each in different directions the effect on the very atmosphere of our community will be as a ripple movement upon the lake. An expansive advancement will cascade outward pulling the broken, hurting and lost in its wake into the Kingdom of God.

Alone, one stone makes it's own impact but as each stone connects to the ripples of others our impact will change a still unmoving community into one filled with shimmering life - the gift of eternal life in Christ.

As a child of the King – let's allow our presence to bring a joyous ripple effect to those around us. For we are His chosen stones and are commissioned to bring the Kingdom of Heaven to those we encounter.

Fall's Yield

Reflections of His Glory

"There's No Place Like Home"

Dorothy landed in Oz with a loud thump of awakening. As she opened the door the overwhelming awareness of not being "in Kansas anymore" rang in her ears as she announced this fact to Toto.

Not being in her familiar surroundings was obvious as we watched the sepia screen erupt with brilliant full color. We too, anticipated her new journey into the unknown.

Her journey toward home began as wisdom was offered – "follow the yellow brick road".

Her travels toward home on this long arduous road quickly began to open her eyes to who she was. Her desire for home quickly showed her how much she had been given and a longing grew that drove her to find this place called home.

Reaching the end of the yellow brick road wasn't the end; for here she didn't find what she expected. More was required to reach her ultimate destination. As she experienced trials and struggles she again comes to the end with nothing in hand.

Disappointment again surges and brings her to tears as finally the true answer is spoken. She finds that her way home was only a "click" away. A very simple statement of faith rang out "There's no place like home" and she was received home with open arms.

Knowing who you are in Christ and that you are always only a "click" away from open arms of love and forgiveness makes your life journey toward home a simple statement of faith.

As you lay down your need to do it all on your own you begin to understand what yielding is all about. A statement of faith and a soft "click, click, click" is where His grace steps in and you are instantly home at His throne.

Your choices are to yield to His outstretched love ("click, click, click") and accept His forgiveness ("There's no place like home").

<u>Decisions on the Yellow Brick Road</u>

Dorothy's yellow brick road had its challenges. Crossroads and voices in this strange land seemed to pop up everywhere.

Periodically her encounter with a crossroad brought her to a place of decision. All roads looked the same but only one would bring her to Oz.

Throughout her journey, Dorothy encountered many voices – a scarecrow, a tin man, a lion, a good witch, munchkins, Oz, the wicked witch and her little Toto. Each one stirred and directed her differently. There were ones of wisdom, love, peace, joy, silent loyalty, fear, anger, manipulation and intimidation. Listening to each of these voices brought either a positive or negative interaction into the story and directed the stories flow on that yellow brick road.

You too, find your life journey peppered with crossroads as well as many voices calling out directions.

Each crossroad you encounter declares a defining moment in your life. The choices made at these times determine your ultimate pre-planned purpose and can affect the rest of your life. If you allow Jesus to BE Lord in those moments you will make it to the end of your journey – your Oz – seeing His amazing faithfulness in all areas.

The voices that inundate your journey and direct your crossroads will ultimately help or hurt you spiritually - not only during those crossroad decision times but also on a daily basis. Learning to listen to only those voices that will strengthen God's plan in your life is a process of choice.

Of those many voices God has placed in your life, many will encourage and direct you with wisdom. However, the ultimate voice to direct your decisions must be the voice of your Lord. Learning that voice means spending time at His feet.

Crossroads will come; voices will speak – BUT only Christ - the one road - will bring you to the place and purpose He has for your life.

Proverbs 8:32-35 – "And now, O sons, listen to me: blessed are those who keep my ways. Hear instruction and be wise, and do not neglect it. Blessed is the one who listens to me, watching daily at my gates, waiting beside my doors. For whoever finds me finds life and obtains favor from the Lord,

Freedom Flows Under His Reign

The resounding thunderous roar of a forceful waterfall erupts over a precipice bringing a surge of awe within our beings.

However, the formation of this mighty eruption begins quite differently. It begins as a trickle.

Over time, that trickle of water strengthens as its determination grows and solidifies its purpose.

Depth and width grow from a trickle, to ankle deep, knee deep, waist deep as its purpose expands. Only then when it is deep enough to swim in does the fun begin. Force begins to operate and the very terrain around it is changed as it makes its path. Often powerfully carving out its way through solid rock.

Its out-pouring and exclamation of freedom and purpose find its expression as it releases all of nature's boundaries and erupts out into its environment bringing life and change.

The free gift of grace poured out to us through Christ is like the formation of a new waterfall. The trickle released to us is His forgiveness. As with parched ground our hearts receive it and we are refreshed. Freedom erupts.

This eruption allows the trickle to grow into a deeper and faster source of water. That growth requires accepting His lordship in our lives. This place opens our eyes and ears to what He has called us to. It shows us the path and directs the way to pass through solid rock.

As we grow from acceptance of grace into a place of Lordship we step into a new place of freedom.

Grace and Lordship release us to walk into a place where the freedom to flow out and cascade with exuberance into His purposes becomes possible. It's a place where we live in freedom under the reign of Christ.

As we live daily walking under His reign we are able to become that resounding thunderous roar of a waterfall as we release all we are created to be into our environment. This is the place we have been called to - the place where heaven touches earth.

Join me as we begin that free flow over the precipice and into the depths of our calling.

II Corinthians 3:17 - Now the Lord is the Spirit, and where the Spirit of the Lord is, there is freedom.

Nature's Nudging

As summer begins its transition to fall nature begins to vibrate with a keen awareness. Trees, flowers, birds and squirrels are all attentively on alert. They have an internal ear that is tuned into changes that need to be heeded as this shift takes place. This awareness is a simple nudging presented by nature.

Leaves begin to shed and petals fall. Birds and squirrels hear the call to prepare in active obedience to natures encouraging love tap and they move into action. Seeds and nuts are diligently gathered and stored. Busyness vibrates in the air as anticipation quivers within.

They listen attentively and in obedience respond to that internal awareness. They obey and do what is needed to prepare for the season.

As we continue our spiritual walk – understanding the grace that Christ's blood provided and placing our lives under His lordship we then begin to hear His voice. Obedience no longer sounds like a demand or expectation. We begin to step under the flow of His reign and attentively listen for His call.

Just as a servant waits at the door expecting to be available to the requests of the King – so should our hearts lean toward that door with anticipation.

Obedience flows from a heart that is saturated in the love and presence of Jesus. Being "sold out" to His directions, plans and purposes allows for the development of a fine tuned ear that hears His call.

Our response is not determined by our own agendas but flows out of love with no hesitation. The call to action brings a quick "Yes Lord".

Join me in the call to action; as we pursue becoming attentive servants who listen and obey our Lords voice from a life filled with abundant love for our Lord and King - Jesus.

John 15:4-5 - Abide in me, and I in you. As the branch cannot bear fruit by itself, unless it abides in the vine, neither can you, unless you abide in me. I am the vine; you are the branches. Whoever abides in me and I in him, he it is that bears much fruit, for apart from me you can do nothing.

1 Peter 1:13 - Therefore, preparing your minds for action, and being sober-minded, set your hope fully on the grace that will be brought to you at the revelation of Jesus Christ.

Nature's Surrender
The Last Lonely Leaves

As the days of fall become shorter and cooler we witness a beautiful example of nature's surrender.

I sit looking out at a grove of enormous maple trees that have provided a canopy of coolness throughout a scorching summer.

Now change is in the air. Cooler breezes and diminishing light begin a new season for the maple. Her leaves surrender to the process as pigment changes begin to dance within each one. Brilliant greens fade into yellows and within days some of those yellows transform to oranges and then reds. Again, over time these vivid beauties give way to browns that quickly signal finality to summer's delight.

The abundance of swaying leaves above will eventually yield to the flight that will land them at our feet. Each of the thousands of leaves will disconnect and yield to this falling process. Each leaf will enter this routine movement at different times and due to different circumstances. The end is always the same. They must end up yielding to natures call to lie down.

As I watch this falling process throughout several weeks I find myself contemplating. Some of the first leaves to let go are still green with just the slightest hints of yellow. They gracefully float to the ground creating the beginning of a soft carpet that will usher in the changes to come.

Then, as time progresses those that are yellow transform into orange and red and are then are shaken lose as winds and rains push and pull them from their previous anchors. They land unceremoniously with a "plop" upon the awaiting soggy ground.

Finally, as the maples nakedness has progressed I see the only leaves left hanging amidst her branches are now brown and dried. However, they still hold on tight. These final leaves refuse to yield to the process. But, the process will prevail.

The next storm approaches and those last lonely leaves are forced to resign to it and in the end they land with a "crunch" on the cold solid ground.

Just as these fall leaves follow a pre-determined yielding process so is there a spiritual yielding process that we experience that can be looked at similarly.

As we are presented with the decision of allowing Jesus the position of "Lordship" in our lives we too must determine how we step into that process. Do we quickly yield – saying "Yes Lord"? Do we take our time "working at it" first? Or do we "hang on" and "fight to the end" before we take that step?

Most of us will find ourselves walking in and out of these processes. So, lets flip this and start this week with the last one.

Let's look at those brown single lonely dried up leaves that are "hanging on" and going to "fight to the end" before they will yield their lives to anyone.

Now, most of you would say, "Oh - that's not me" but think again.

Whether you have been in or out of church your whole life you have heard the mind set that our society touts as beneficial in order to be a strong independent individual —we don't give up, we fight to the end, we don't need any help, and on and on it goes. So if you have grown up with that thinking, then the process of totally yielding to anyone – including Jesus can be a complete paradigm shift for you.

Many of us think we have already yielded to Jesus when we accepted Him as savior but often we have held back from the completeness of that salvation by hanging onto the branches of our previous tree. Meaning that our old thoughts and ways have continued to influence our Christian life.

Often we are so caught up in our own lives that we have become dried up and brittle. Our spirituality consists of maybe hearing a sermon once a week and going through the motions the rest of the week.

We are walking a life that is far from His desire. We don't live a life where Christ is reigning in our lives in freedom because we are not allowing HIS LORDSHIP in our life.

Our ways, our desires, our wants, our needs, our offenses - these and many others are all pieces of who we are and they need to come under HIS LORDSHIP.

His grace paid for it all – we don't need to carry any of it and we can't control anything anyways so why not just say "Yes, Lord" and let all of - Our Stuff - go. His Grace + His Lordship = complete freedom and a yielded moldable life ready to be poured out.

Let's allow the mindset of "hang on" and "fight to the end" to be released at the feet of Jesus.

Proverbs 3:5-6   - Trust in the LORD with all your heart, and do not lean on your own understanding. In all your ways acknowledge him, and he will make straight your paths.

Nature's Surrender
Those "Holding On" to Full Color

The grand display of colors that present themselves to us as the beauty of fall unfolds now brings us back to contemplate the changing color process.

By the time we see the bright orange and reds of our maple tree she has already lost many leaves that yielded earlier.

These that are now present are the leaves who have gone through the summer, adjusted to the yellowing and now have embraced full on color change and are holding on and walking through it all.

As we apply a spiritual comparison remember our desire is for surrendering at the feet of Jesus.

We are looking at a brilliant leaf that has accepted its place, its position, its role and it is walking and working just as expected in order to complete what it was set up for. Right? Right.

BUT – that's the snag!

At first thought these brilliant colorful leaves would be my preference to be. However, learning to walk under the true Lordship of Christ requires something different.

We have been taught both in and out of the church to "find your place, find your role and work hard to achieve" Work, work, work and more work.

However, what we accomplish or don't accomplish doesn't matter to Jesus. He already loved you so much that He gave his life for you and there is nothing that will change that. You do NOT earn anything by working or doing anything for Him. He doesn't need anything from you.

Once you understand that place of undeserved favor – called grace; then you can accept Him and place Him in a position of Lordship over your life where with joy and freedom you will move into a new place. Here your only desire is to hear and obey when He speaks.

Let's take time to lie down all the "busyness". Let's stop "working" to prove anything. Now let's surrender to the process of making Jesus the Lord over our life.

Nature's Surrender
Early Yielders

With the first cooling breeze of fall begins a rustle in the waiting leaves of our maple trees. An anticipation of what is to come wiggles at the tips and stems of the leaves that expectantly wait for the first call. The first breeze lifts several leaves as they willingly detach from the limbs of the maples outstretched arms. With amazing grace they flutter unhindered through the air and land with a soft release as the beginning of fall's carpet quietly materializes.

As we again apply a spiritual comparison between these leaves and our lives - let's consider our own willingness to surrender.

Waiting and anticipation require a process of listening, which requires a place of quiet.

Willingness to step into a place with expectation is part of the acceptance of surrender.

Just as these first leaves of fall take flight we must be ready and anticipate His call. That type of yielding comes from a place of trusting Him beyond all others and knowing His voice when He calls.

Join me as we willingly detach and lie down in full surrender to His call.

The Woodpeckers Single Focus

The early fall morning awakens to the encroaching fog that shrouds the day with stillness and an atmosphere of peace.

Interruption begins as a distinct "tap, tap, tap" beckons for attention.

The previous stillness gives way to this persistent sound.

Hearing the abrupt repetitive wood taping sound reverberating in a consistent cycle of three "tap, tap, tap"s begins to draw me into a search for this lone woodpecker.

The resounding cycle continues, seeming to fill the entire valley with its declaration of presence.

Searching tree to tree I finally see our little driller. This little red headed culprit takes no notice of me for I am not his concern.

This lone woodpecker has a single focus and purpose. To establish and declare his territory as well as attracting appropriate attention for his ultimate design. These purposes are clearly set before him.

This little guy has a single focus and declaration to pursue the call that nature instilled within him and he is a great example of God's plan for you.

102

As you walk daily under the Lordship and reign of Christ your focus will become singular. The voice of your Lord will begin to resound within you as He directs your purpose. The establishing of His territory in your life, through your life and into others lives will become a declaration of His Kingdom.

Join me as we become like the woodpecker with a single focus yielded and moldable to His purposes.

Proverbs 3:5-6 - Trust in the LORD with all your heart, and do not lean on your own understanding. In all your ways acknowledge him, and he will make straight your paths.

Hebrews 11:1 - Now faith is the assurance of things hoped for, the conviction of things not seen.

Yield to the Call and Open the Door

You stand looking in from the outside at this house made of glass. The winds begin to howl and rains splash coldly over your head. You can see the huge glowing rock fireplace with a roaring crackling fire within its hearth. You know it will be warm and dry inside. You know that you have access to its presence. The choice is up to you. It only requires you to open the door.

The choice is made and the door glides open as a whole new adventure materializes before you. What you thought is nothing like it is. There is warmth beyond imagination. The sound of the fire that you had never heard now crackles and sizzles igniting your senses. The smell you could never have experienced before now swirls around your head as smoke and wood meld together in this new atmosphere.

All that you thought you understood about this experience has now exploded into a new inexpressible encounter at the feet of Jesus.

Have you come into this house? Have you chosen to open the door?

Whether you have never known Jesus or have been in or out of the church for years that door can be opened with a simple choice.

104

Many of you within the church for a lifetime have continued to stand on the outside of this glass house. Looking longingly at the fire, thinking you understand it but never partaking of all that is there and offered to you free of charge.

Don't wait – yield to the call to open that door and walk into a new life free to enjoy all that He has already paid for just for you. Walk into a NEW experience at the feet of Jesus as the Holy Spirit opens your eyes to His presence.

James 1:17 - Every good gift and every perfect gift is from above, coming down from the Father of lights with whom there is no variation or shadow due to change.

Revelation 3:20 - Behold, I stand at the door and knock. If anyone hears my voice and opens the door, I will come in to him and eat with him, and he with me.

Let Him Sweep Up the Mess

Let's watch as a neighbor begins a remodeling process of his yard and drive way.

First comes the "un-doing".

The jackhammers begin to vibrate the area as breaking through the previously poured concrete begins. The air continues to resound with the process - as the pounding of hammers joins in the crescendo. Next comes the bringing down of the block walled fencing with thuds and shacking of the earth. Trucks arrive with backhoes and added helpers as the tearing and ripping out of the old shrubs and grass joins the process.

Days of noise continue to fill the previously quiet street. The once familiar view is now in chaos as activity reigns.

Suddenly, one morning we awake to silence once again. Upon looking - the dust has settled but what is viewed now is a yard full of rubble. The day continues in silence and when day two gives silently away to the sound of crickets we began to wonder. "Is it possible they have no plans for re-building?"

As the sun begins to warm the dust on the third morning we find one silent worker – the neighbor – with a broom and a wheelbarrow. He works diligently all day clearing all the brokenness that has been accomplished during the de-construction phase.

Let's ponder this process. We too require an "un-doing" phase in our lives as well as a clean up and re-building.

During our spiritual life journey we encounter hurts and offences, which cause us to build walls of protection that surround our hearts. Those offences and hurts can be legitimate and some trivial but the walls become thicker and thicker as time moves on.

In order to be free and totally yielded to the call of Christ in our lives we must be willing to set all of these offences and hurts down. This requires an "un-doing" of walls and cracked foundations.

What takes days in the natural only takes a yielded heart in the spiritual. Acknowledging these hurts and offences and being willing to allow the tearing down process to begin will transform your life. You will begin to be free to open up to others, let them in and see a future that was previously hidden behind those walls.

Don't allow fear of "the clean-up" to stop you and keep you hidden behind those walls. It is only your job to say "Yes Lord". He has the broom and wheelbarrow and lovingly will sweep up the mess.

Believe in His Faithfulness

Once the clean up of our neighbors yard is complete workers again converge. This time the focus is on the foundation of the driveway. Frames are placed and cement begins to flow. Time and patience is required as the process continues. Curing is temperamental and it will be many days before it can be tested with any weight. Again our street sits silent for days waiting to see how this project will emerge.   No activity.   No movement.   Just anticipation.

Finally, one morning as our blinds are raised we stand stunned by our new view. What yesterday was barren is new today. The sun glistens off of dewy blades of grass and beautifully manicured shrubs and trees in our neighbors yard.

"How can that be?" we question. "These things don't just happen, they take hard work".

We see but don't believe. In fairy-tales and magic shows we see things appear and disappear. When the stunning assistant is covered with a black bag and placed into a locked chest she now instantly disappears. What was a pumpkin and mice becomes a carriage and beautiful stallions. We see but don't believe. We believe in masters of illusion and special affects.

Looking at our spiritual walk we expect that hard work is required from us to achieve any change. We must do it.

However, once our choice to say "Yes Lord" takes place Christ steps in and cleans up the mess of our lives.

A new foundation begins. This foundation does take some time, some patience and trusting in the process. But all the glory comes as He unveils what was hidden inside of you. The fresh laid grass and beautifully manicured shrubs appear. The pumpkin and mice DO instantly become something new. The box that was once filled of our sins, hurts and offences IS empty.

Our willingness to yield to His Lordship brings His reign – His yield of abundance and change into our lives.

Allow this process in your life to materialize as you daily walk under His reign and watch as old things become new – Believe in His faithfulness.

II Corinthians 3:18 – And we all, with unveiled face, beholding the glory of the Lord, are being transformed into the same image from one degree of glory to another. For this comes from the Lord who is the Spirit.

<u>Abundant Fruit Happens in a Yielded Life</u>

Fall brings with it a natural yielding process full of abundant goodness as we look forward to the harvesting of its provision.

With love and care the gardener has watered, fertilized, pruned and prepared throughout the warm summer months. His focus and attention has been in anticipation for what will be produced upon his vines and trees as fall approaches.

As his vines and fruit trees grow heavy with abundant fruit, preparation to consume and preserve their bounty kicks into high gear all around him. The sheer joy of the overflowing fragrant ripeness of these fruits permeates and stirs us to action. We climb, gather, wash, sort and share as we look forward to pies to be made, jams to be canned and juices to be squeezed.

We enjoy the bounty that is poured forth from the hand of the gardener who has done all the cultivating for our benefit. What an abundant blessing of His yield has been given to us!

Spiritually, we have a master gardener who has done the watering, fertilizing, pruning and preparing. Watching and waiting for the fruit to burst forth in our lives.

As we yield to His Lordship and live under His reign – fruit happens.

We yield to Him and He pours an abundant yield into and through our lives.

Join me as we enjoy and share those fruits – being ready to pour them out to everyone we encounter.

II Corinthians 2:14-17 - But thanks be to God, who in Christ always leads us in triumphal procession, and through us spreads the fragrance of the knowledge of him everywhere. For we are the aroma of Christ to God among those who are being saved and among those who are perishing, to one a fragrance from death to death, to the other a fragrance from life to life. Who is sufficient for these things? For we are not, like so many, peddlers of God's word, but as men of sincerity, as commissioned by God, in the sight of God we speak in Christ.

Galatians 2:20 - I have been crucified with Christ. It is no longer I who live, but Christ who lives in me. And the life I now live in the flesh I live by faith in the Son of God, who loved me and gave himself for me.

The Faithful Evergreen's Canopy

As fall commences the barren trees and vines lapse into sleep as the season approaches. However, the evergreen fir continues to declare her-self. Nature's now bleak landscape is vibrant and alive because of her presence just as every season before. She provides a canopy in every region from the ocean to the desert.

Year after year the evergreen stands as a sentry on a wall. Her innate knowledge of natures design buried deep within. She pours out to us a gift that is often enjoyed and received with no acknowledgment.

The evergreen yields as season after season passes.

Winter covers her with frost and snow, as well as biting winds that bend and rip at her branches. Spring brings new life as many birds enjoy her outstretched support and protection as nests of babies flourish. Summer rushes in with beating unrelenting sun and heat. But the evergreen stands strong bringing shade to humans and animals alike. Fall begins and gives relief to her as rains begin to pour forth and she yields to their refreshing.

Even through disasters – fires, landslides and more - those you see still standing often are the branchless, charred and bent – stately, faithful, yielding evergreens.

Similarly, we desire to walk through our spiritual life journey declaring the same.

Our faith in Christ and His design for our lives is our primary focus. As we trust in the invisible – we begin to know that He is always for us. His love draws us to a place where our desire to be who we are created to be gives rise within us to pour out that love back to our "daddy". Knowing who we are in Him grows that desire not to present anything back to Him out of obligation but because we love Him so much we want to make Him smile. We no longer need to be noticed by others but do what He directs and that is what drives our lives.

We begin to allow our branches to carry the frost, snow and winds both for ourselves and for others. We lift up life and speak encouragement always. We stand in faith as the heat scorches. We bring shade to those we encounter and love. As fall approaches we yield again to His call and His direction. Year after year growing stronger and deeper in faith. We are always ready for the next season.

The yielding process is not one that occurs once and is done. It is a life journey that begins and continues to grow as we willingly set aside our ways and accept His. Listening to His voice and season after season we stand on that voice.

Join me in this amazing journey - where it is always MORE of Him and LESS of me.

1 Corinthians 15:58 - Therefore, my beloved brothers, be steadfast, immovable, always abounding in the work of the Lord, knowing that in the Lord your labor is not in vain.

Isaiah 61: 1-6 - The Spirit of the Lord God is upon me, because the Lord has anointed me to bring good news to the poor; he has sent me to bind up the brokenhearted, to proclaim liberty to the captives,
and the opening of the prison to those who are bound; to proclaim the year of the Lord's favor, and the day of vengeance of our God; to comfort all who mourn; to grant to those who mourn in Zion—
to give them a beautiful headdress instead of ashes, the oil of gladness instead of mourning, the garment of praise instead of a faint spirit; that they may be called oaks of righteousness, the planting of the Lord, that he may be glorified. They shall build up the ancient ruins; they shall raise up the former devastations; they shall repair the ruined cities, the devastations of many generations. Strangers shall stand and tend your flocks; foreigners shall be your plowmen and vinedressers; but you shall be called the priests of the Lord; they shall speak of you as the ministers of our God; you shall eat the wealth of the nations, and in their glory you shall boast.

Galatians 6:9-10 - And let us not grow weary of doing good, for in due season we will reap, if we do not give up. So then, as we have opportunity, let us do good to everyone, and especially to those who are of the household of faith.

<u>Notes</u>

<u>Note</u>

Titles available by J.K. Sanchez

Majestic Reflection Devotional Study Series:

Winters Rest

Spring's Assurance

Summer's Delight

Fall's Yield

Stand alone or companion journals:

Winters Rest Journal

Spring's Assurance Journal

Summer's Delight Journal

Fall's Yield Journal

Majestic Reflection Journal

Reflections of His Glory Journal

Additional Titles

Reflections of His Glory

Contact me at: Judy@jksanchez.com

Jksanchez.com

25

<u>About the Author</u>

J. K. Sanchez has lived and raised her three children in the Pacific Northwest where she and her husband of 40 years live and enjoy its beauty. As a writer and photographer her love of nature has flourished and is portrayed both through visually descriptive prose as well as through the eye of the camera.

Having ministered in many areas of the body of Christ her love for people and passion for worship and the presence of the Lord continually draw her to see freedom proclaimed and released to others through the finished work on the cross of Jesus.

www.ingramcontent.com/pod-product-compliance
Lightning Source LLC
Chambersburg PA
CBHW060311050426
42448CB00009B/1789